The INSIDE GUIDE

MOVEMENTS FOR EQUALITY

The Story of the Native American Rights Movement

By Sophie Washburne

Cavendish Square

Published in 2024 by Cavendish Square Publishing, LLC
2544 Clinton Street Buffalo, NY 14224

Website: cavendishsq.com

Library of Congress Cataloging-in-Publication Data

Names: Washburne, Sophie, author.
Title: The story of the Native American rights movement / Sophie Washburne.
Description: Buffalo, NY : Cavendish Square Publishing, [2024] | Series: The inside guide : movements for equality | Includes bibliographical references and index.
Identifiers: LCCN 2023012740 | ISBN 9781502668080 (library binding) | ISBN 9781502668073 (paperback) | ISBN 9781502668097 (ebook)
Subjects: LCSH: Indians of North America–Government relations–Juvenile literature. | Indians of North America–Politics and government–Juvenile literature. | American Indian Movement–Juvenile literature. | Indians of North America–Civil rights–Juvenile literature. | Indians, Treatment of–United States–Juvenile literature.
Classification: LCC E93 .W28 2024 | DDC 323.1197–dc23/eng/20230407
LC record available at https://lccn.loc.gov/2023012740

Editor: Jennifer Lombardo
Copyeditor: Michele Suchomel-Casey
Designer: Claire Wrazin

The photographs in this book are used by permission and through the courtesy of: Cover courtesy of the Library of Congress; p. 4 Peter Hermes Furian/Shutterstock.com; p. 6 (left) Shannon Dunaway/Shutterstock.com; p. 6 (right) Paul Cash/Shutterstock.com; p. 7 File:Mystic Massacre 1637 Destruction Of The Pequots in Connecticut.png/Wikimedia Commons; p. 9 Daria Perevezentsev/Shutterstock.com; p. 10 DCSHUTT/Shutterstock.com; p. 13 (left) KOTOIMAGES/Shutterstock.com; p. 13 (right) Andreas Stroh/Shutterstock.com; p. 14 Sean Linehan/National Oceanic and Atmospheric Administration; p. 16 Associated Press/APNewsroom; p. 18 SvetlanaSF/Shutterstock.com; p. 19 Marzolino/Shutterstock.com; p. 21 MintImages/Shutterstock.com; p. 22 Ben Hovland/Shutterstock.com; p. 24 arindambanerjee/Shutterstock.com; p. 25 File:Pine Ridge - Osawatomie 2.JPG/Wikimedia Commons; p. 27 Liam Hill-Allan/Shutterstock.com; p. 29 (left) Courtesy of the U.S. National Archives and Records Administration; p. 29 (middle) Rena Schild/Shutterstock.com; p. 29 (right) Margarita Young/Shutterstock.com.

CPSIA compliance information: Batch #CSCSQ24: For further information contact Cavendish Square Publishing LLC at 1-877-980-4450.

Printed in the United States of America

CONTENTS

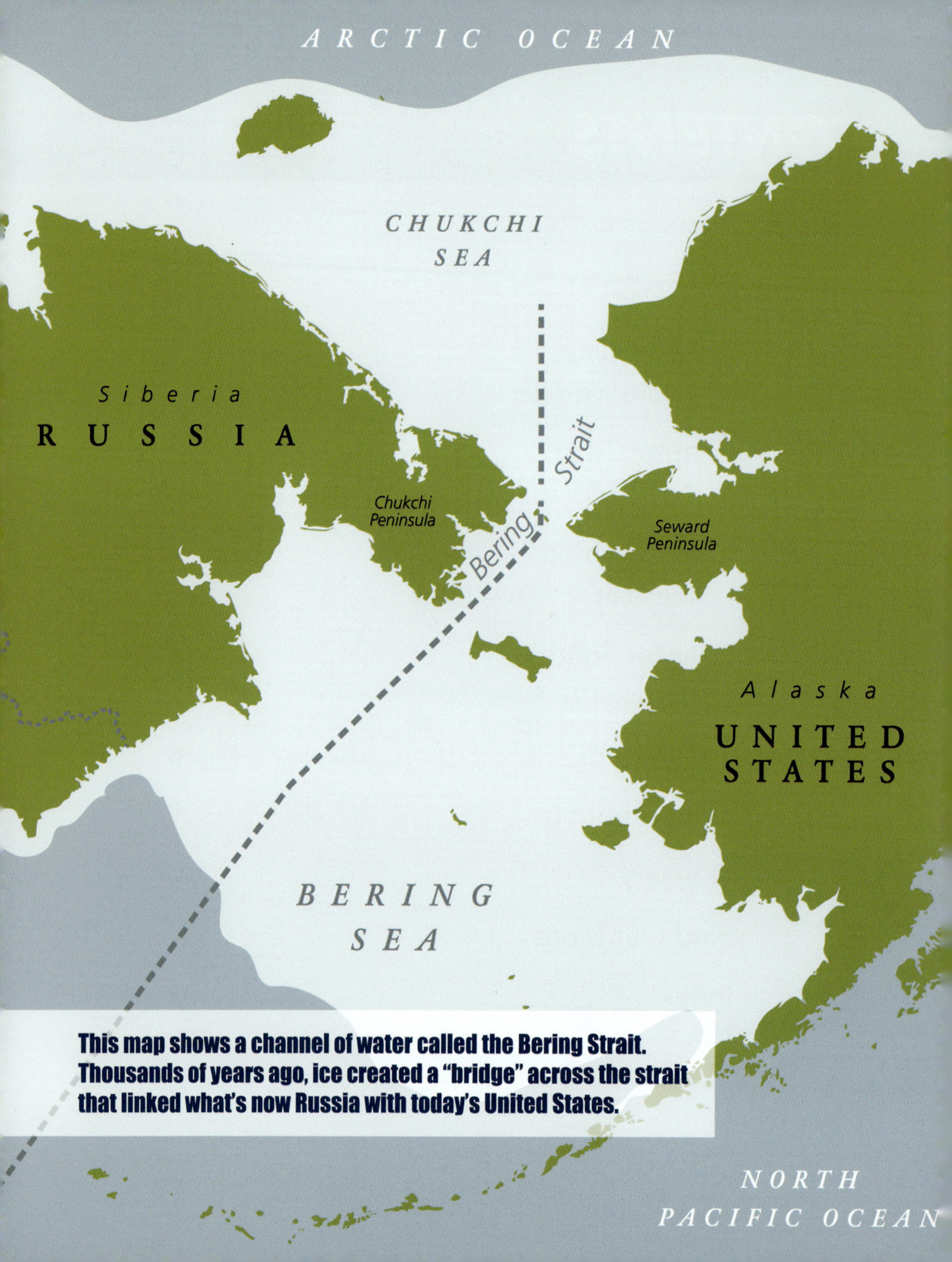

This map shows a channel of water called the Bering Strait. Thousands of years ago, ice created a "bridge" across the strait that linked what's now Russia with today's United States.

BEFORE AND AFTER

Chapter One

Native Americans have lived in North America for close to 18,000 years. Many experts believe the first people to come to the Americas crossed a land bridge from Asia and settled across the continent. This group of people lost contact with each other over time and broke into hundreds of separate groups. These people were the first to occupy the Americas.

While Native Americans may share common **ancestors**, each group has its own culture, or set of traditions, beliefs, and ways of life. For thousands of years, tribal nations had their own systems of government and social order. Life existed this way for most cultures until the 15th century, when Europeans crossed an ocean to lay claim to the land.

Violence and Destruction

Life for Native Americans changed forever after Europeans arrived. The Europeans brought horses, guns, and sicknesses such as smallpox. Thousands of **Indigenous** people died from these unfamiliar threats. As the Europeans established colonies, they pushed Indigenous people off the land they had lived on for years. Often, they did this violently. Some Indigenous people fought back and were killed. Others signed **treaties** with the invaders.

Different Indigenous groups had different ways of living. For example, the Haudenosaunee, also known as the Iroquois, lived in longhouses like the one shown on the right. Plains Indians, such as the Apache and Blackfoot, lived in tipis similar to the one shown on the left.

Fast Fact

Today, only about 3 percent of the U.S. population is Native American.

Many treaties stated that Native American groups would give up their land in exchange for smaller areas of land west of the Mississippi River. These pieces of land were called reservations. Some groups were forced to sign treaties, while others made the decision on their own, hoping to protect themselves from further violence. However, the government often broke treaties, especially if the land the Indigenous people had been given was found

INCORRECT NAMES

When Christopher Columbus landed in the Caribbean in 1492, he mistakenly believed he had reached India. For that reason, he called the Indigenous people he met "Indians." The term stuck, and some still use "American Indian" today to talk about themselves. Others prefer "Native American" or "Indigenous" to refer to the group as a whole.

When speaking to or about an individual, most people prefer to be called by the name of their specific culture, such as Cherokee or Inuit. This is similar to the way we might talk about Europeans as a whole but Italians or Greeks as members of individual cultures.

This picture shows European colonizers massacring an Indigenous group called the Pequots in 1637.

to be valuable in some way. The wars and treaties slowly stripped away their power and freedoms. In time, Native Americans became a minority group in the land that first belonged to them.

Bad Conditions

The U.S. government began establishing reservations after 1778. Throughout the 1800s, millions of Native Americans were forcibly removed from their lands and relocated to lands in what are now the states of Oklahoma, South Dakota, and Arizona, as well as other territories in the West. Conditions on reservations have historically been poor. People suffered from lack of food, proper clothing, and housing. They didn't receive the resources and support they were promised. Things are better now than they were in the past, but reservations still have much higher **poverty** rates than the rest of the country.

> **Fast Fact**
>
> There often is not enough housing for everyone on reservations, and the houses that are available are often not in good condition. The schools often don't have enough money and tend to be overcrowded.

Native Americans have also been forced to assimilate to, or fit in with, white society. Between 1880 and 1925, as many as 60,000 Native American children were removed from their homes and forced to attend boarding schools that were often thousands of miles away. They weren't allowed to speak their native language, practice their traditional beliefs, or wear traditional clothing. They were given new names and forced to learn how to fit in with white society.

In many schools, the children had to deal with physical and emotional abuse. Many even died and were buried in unmarked graves on the

Each pair of shoes in this photo represents an Indigenous child who was killed at Kamloops Indian Residential School in British Columbia, Canada.

Fast Fact

In 2021, news broke that more than 600 children's bodies had been found at the site of an Indigenous boarding school in Canada. Since then, thousands of similar unmarked graves have been found across North America.

grounds; their families were never told. This form of **discrimination** separated Native American children from their families and homes in an attempt to erase their true cultural identity. These boarding schools had mostly closed by 1969, but their effects are still felt today.

Some reservations, such as this Navajo reservation in Arizona, are far from other towns. If the reservation doesn't have something, it can be hard for people to go somewhere else to get it, especially if they don't own a car.

Chapter Two

GETTING ORGANIZED

In large part because of the problems of reservation life, Indigenous people were more likely than the rest of the U.S. population to suffer from serious sicknesses, especially alcoholism and diabetes. Many people were unwilling to hire them, so they also had difficulty finding jobs that paid well. This meant that many Indigenous people lived in poverty even outside reservations.

Formal resistance to these conditions began during World War II (1939–1945). The National Congress of American Indians (NCAI) formed in 1944 to protect Indigenous rights and improve educational opportunities and standards of living for their people.

Fast Fact

Native Americans weren't allowed to vote until 1924, even though many Indigenous men had joined the U.S. Army and fought in wars before then.

One Step Forward, Two Steps Back

After years of outright violence, the U.S. government began taking steps toward treating Indigenous people more fairly. For example, in 1934, the government passed the Indian Reorganization Act. This law was meant to stop people from taking more Indigenous lands. It also set

Fast Fact

Like Black and Hispanic students, Native American students were segregated, or kept separate from white students. The schools that served these groups were underfunded and overcrowded, so they didn't provide as good of an education as white-only schools.

aside some money to improve life on the reservations.

In 1952, the U.S. government launched the Urban Indian Relocation Program. On its surface, it sounded good. The program encouraged Native Americans to move to major cities to find jobs. They were promised housing, money, job training, and other resources. However, the housing was poor and there were fewer jobs and educational opportunities than they'd been led to believe. It was also around this time that the U.S. government stopped legally recognizing many groups. This meant they no longer qualified to receive the money that had been set aside for them by the Indian Reorganization Act.

Life in cities was very different from life on the reservations, and many Native Americans had a hard time adjusting to their new environment. They felt homesick. They also experienced discrimination nearly everywhere they went. In some cities, police targeted public places where many Native Americans gathered.

Fast Fact

Native American people are 1.2 times more likely to be killed by police than Black people are. While the Black Lives Matter movement has gotten huge attention, the same issue has largely been overlooked when it comes to Native Americans.

Taking a Stand

Ever since the first Europeans had arrived in North America, Indigenous

When many white people think of Native Americans, they picture people living a traditional way of life. However, most Native Americans live just like the rest of the U.S. population. In fact, for many years, traditional Indigenous cultural practices were illegal.

people had been fighting back. These resistance efforts were generally done by individual people or groups. For example, from 1957 to 1959, the Tuscarora of New York blocked the state government's attempt to turn their reservation land into a reservoir, or man-made lake. Tuscarora women led much of the resistance, blocking construction equipment with their bodies and removing poles that had been placed into the ground to mark the construction site.

Fishing has been an important part of many Indigenous cultures for thousands of years. After the Europeans arrived, these groups had to fight to keep this part of their culture alive.

CIVIL DISOBEDIENCE

Civil disobedience, or protesting by breaking unfair laws, has been used by many activists over the years to create change. One form of civil disobedience used by an activist group called the Survival of the American Indian Society (SAIA) was called a "fish-in." This was similar to a sit-in, where activists sit in a public place and refuse to move until their demands are met.

Throughout the 20th century, states in the Pacific Northwest attempted to ignore treaties that granted Indigenous people the right to hunt and fish on and off reservation land. In the 1960s and 1970s, SAIA members exercised their treaty rights by disobeying fishing laws.

In the 1960s, Native Americans began to create organizations that brought together **activists** from multiple Indigenous cultures. One of these was the National Indian Youth Council. Known for their **militant** behavior, members of this group organized protests, demonstrations, and marches. This group was the first to use the phrase "Red Power." This was inspired by the Black Power movement, which was a militant movement around the same time that fought for rights and political power for Black people.

Shown here are members of the American Indian Movement (AIM) protesting by occupying a government building in 1972.

Chapter Three

THE START OF A MOVEMENT

In cities, people from many different Native American cultures united to talk about their ideas and beliefs. Soon, they banded together in the spirit of political activism. Multiple Native American activist groups were formed in the 1960s and 1970s. Some of their actions were directly inspired by the actions Black Americans were taking around the same time as they fought their own civil rights battle.

Keeping Indigenous People Safe

The American Indian Movement (AIM) was first created to help Native Americans who had been relocated by the Urban Indian Relocation Program. AIM members fought back against racism and police brutality, or extreme violence, in Minneapolis, Minnesota. They followed police officers and filmed them as they attacked and arrested Native Americans. AIM members worked to make sure that Native Americans were treated fairly by police officers, or helped them avoid police altogether.

Fast Fact

AIM was founded by Ojibwe people, but it was open to all Indigenous cultures. One of the group's most notable speakers, Russell Means, was an Oglala Lakota Sioux.

THE AMERICAN INDIAN MOVEMENT

AIM was the best-known activist group. It was founded in Minneapolis in July 1968 by several Ojibwe people: Dennis Banks, George Mitchell, Clyde Bellecourt, Pat Bellanger, and Eddie Benton Banai. The group worked to address problems Native Americans faced, including discrimination in the courts and denial of their treaty rights. AIM members believed that being militant was the only way to make the U.S. government listen to their concerns. Within two years after it was founded, AIM had about 5,000 members. There were 79 chapters by 1973, making it a national organization.

These buttons show AIM's logo, or symbol. They also say "Remember Wounded Knee." This was the place where the U.S. Army massacred nearly 300 Lakota people in 1890.

For thousands of years, hunting has been an important part of many Native American cultures. They have fought to keep this and other traditions alive since the Europeans arrived in North America.

As AIM grew, it expanded its efforts. It hosted marches, protests, and sit-ins to draw attention to unfair treatment of Native Americans. The group worked to improve housing for Indigenous people and helped families move. It also started a radio program and a newsletter, and the leaders presented programs at conferences. In 1972, AIM helped found community schools in Minneapolis and Saint Paul, Minnesota. The Heart of the Earth Survival School and Red School House were environments where students could learn about Indigenous cultures, including their languages and traditional practices.

A Long Occupation

In 1969, a Mohawk man named Richard Oakes organized a group of Native Americans to occupy, or take over and live on, Alcatraz Island in California's San Francisco Bay. Because the group was made up of people from different Indigenous cultures, they called themselves Indians of All Tribes. On November 20, this group of about 100 activists arrived on the island and claimed it for Native Americans. Most of them were college students.

The occupiers had a few goals in mind. They wanted the deed, or legal rights, to the island, which had been occupied by Indigenous people for thousands of years before it became part of the United States. They also wanted to create a Native American university, museum, and cultural center on the island. Ultimately, they wanted to show the world that Native Americans needed **self-determination**.

The occupation of Alcatraz Island lasted for 19 months. In the beginning, there was a lot of cooperation among the occupiers. However, as time went on, some people left and new ones arrived. The newcomers didn't always want to follow Oakes's leadership, and some started their own groups that tried to take control. Additionally, the government cut off the island's electricity and freshwater supplies.

The occupation ended on June 10, 1971, when President Richard Nixon ordered government officials to remove the 15 people who remained on the island. Although the occupiers didn't achieve all their goals, the protest had not been for nothing. It brought the public's attention to the issues Indigenous people faced in the United States. The actions of the occupiers also caused the government to create an official policy of self-determination and to stop disbanding tribes. Furthermore, during the time of the occupation, Nixon returned 48,000 acres (19,425 hectares) of land in California to the Taos people.

A prison was built on Alcatraz Island in 1934. It closed in 1963, six years before the occupation organized by Oakes.

Native American protests continue today. In this photo, police face protesters who pulled down a statue of Christopher Columbus in St. Paul, Minnesota, in 2020.

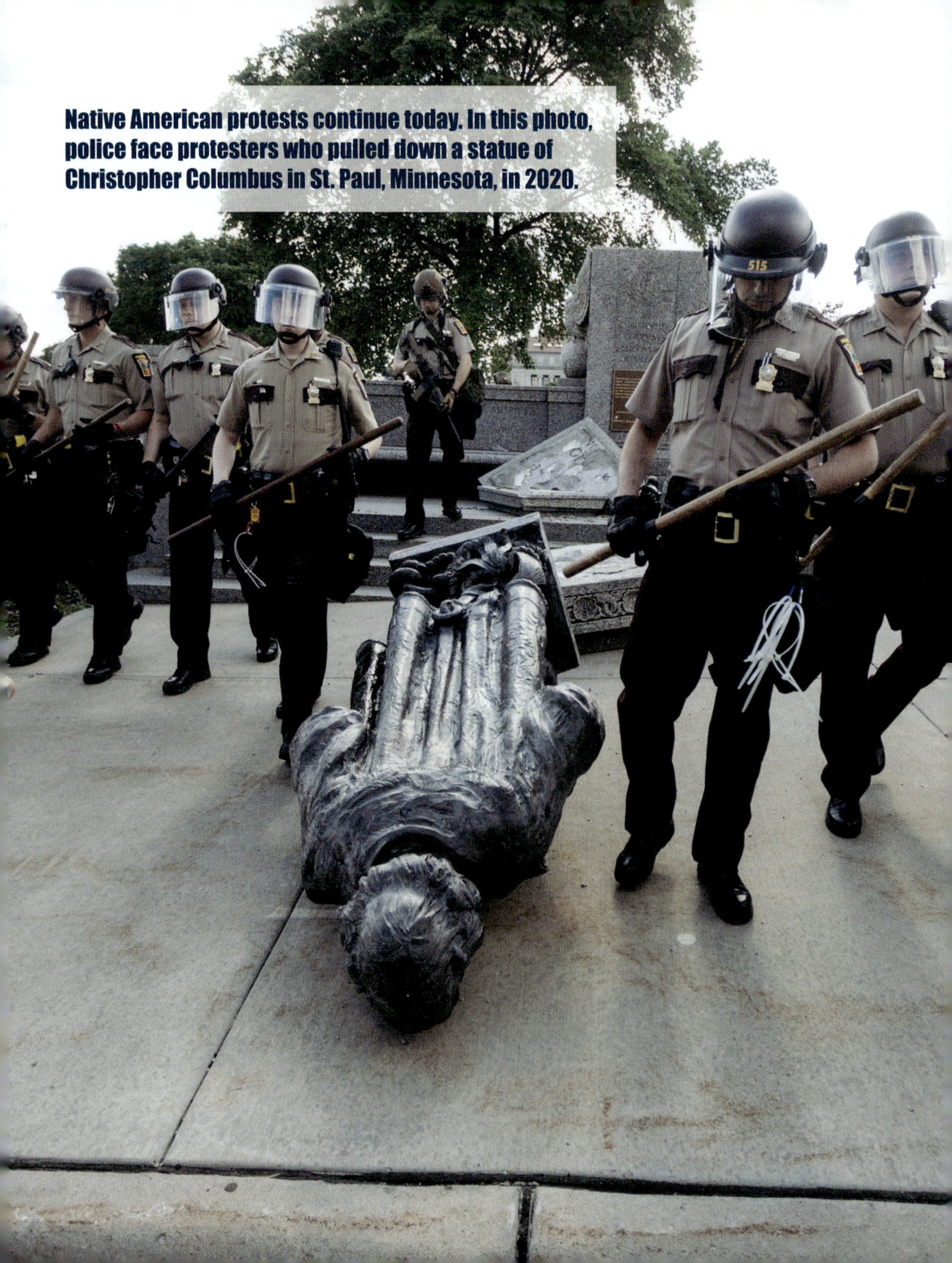

MORE TO DO

Chapter Four

The occupation of Alcatraz and its success in getting the government to create a policy of self-determination showed Native American activists that direct confrontation—forcing the government and the American public to stop ignoring them—was the only way to get things done. The movement was picking up steam across the country in the early 1970s, making Native Americans more determined than ever to achieve their goals. One of these goals was to force the U.S. government to follow the treaties it had signed in the past with Native American governing bodies.

Fast Fact

The Twenty Points Position Paper was a document activists created that outlined 20 demands they had for the U.S. government. These included following treaties, returning stolen land, and changing the way tribes were governed.

The Trail of Broken Treaties

In October 1972, eight activist groups—including AIM, SAIA, and Indians of All Tribes—joined forces to create a mass movement. Large groups of Native Americans set out from Washington State, California, and Oklahoma, bound

Native American activists and allies, or supporters, are still working today to get the U.S. and Canadian governments to keep the promises they made when they signed treaties.

Fast Fact

The group that set out from Oklahoma retraced the path the Cherokee took on the Trail of Tears. This was meant to remind non-Natives of what the government had done.

for Washington, D.C. These groups traveled across the country, stopping at reservations along the way to listen to other Native Americans to take their concerns to the president. This **demonstration** was called the Trail of Broken Treaties. This was a reference to the Trail of Tears, in which the U.S. government forced the

OCCUPY WOUNDED KNEE

In the 1970s, political unrest broke out on the Pine Ridge Indian Reservation in South Dakota. A group of traditional Oglala Lakota people wanted a tribal leader to be removed from office, but he refused to step down. To try to remove him by force, AIM members occupied the village of Wounded Knee starting on February 27, 1973.

The U.S. government sent the National Guard to end the occupation. They cut off the town's electricity and water, and both sides shot at each other daily. When an Oglala man named Buddy Lamont was shot and killed, the Oglala Lakota started working with the government so no one else would die. The occupation ended on May 8.

This poster asked non-Natives to support AIM's occupation of Wounded Knee.

Cherokee to walk from their tribal lands in the South to a reservation in Oklahoma in the 1830s. Many have called this an act of **genocide**.

When the activists arrived in Washington, D.C., government officials wouldn't meet with them, so they occupied the building that housed the

Bureau of Indian Affairs—the government agency responsible for making the laws that affect Native Americans. The occupation brought national attention, both positive and negative, to the cause. The protesters received $66,000 for travel costs, and the government said it would read their Twenty Points Position Paper.

Not Giving Up

Native American activist groups fought hard for change. Because of their work, important legislation was passed, such as the Indian Civil Rights Act (1968), Indian Education Act (1972), and Indian Health Care Improvement Act (1976). They turned a national spotlight on American Indian people and the issues their communities face. Their work influenced policy change at the federal level.

Fast Fact

The Wounded Knee occupation was AIM's last big protest. Today, the group is smaller and concentrates mostly on lobbying, or convincing lawmakers to pass laws that will help Native Americans.

However, the fight is not over. Native Americans still face many hardships today, including poverty, lack of education and economic opportunities, and health challenges. Racism, discrimination, and violence are realities too. Native American people, especially men, are more likely to be killed by police than any other group in the United States and Canada.

Native American women are more likely than any other group to experience physical violence, including murder. A movement called Missing and Murdered Indigenous Women and Girls (MMWIG) is working to bring awareness to this issue and to stop the violence.

A handprint across the mouth—often done in red or orange paint—is MMWIG's symbol. This photo was taken at an MMWIG awareness march in Vancouver, Canada, in 2019.

Native Americans' struggles are often ignored by non-Natives, so the first step is raising awareness. Activists hope to inspire others to believe that it's the responsibility of all Americans to fight for the rights of Native Americans.

TRIBAL LANDS

Present-Day State	Cultures
California	Chafan, Mattole, Molalla, Nongatl, Sinkyone, Tututni, Wailaki
New York	Haudenosaunee, Mohawk, Montaukett, Onondaga, Setalcott, Tuscarora, Wenrohronon
Florida	Ais, Calusa, Guacata, Matecumbe, Miccosukee, Seminole, Tequesta, Timucua

This chart shows just a few Native American cultures and where they lived before the Europeans arrived.

THINK ABOUT IT!

1. Why do you think the Europeans were so violent toward the Native Americans?
2. What actions could the U.S. government have taken to be fair to Native Americans?
3. Why do you think Native Americans wanted a policy of self-determination?
4. How can you help raise awareness of the issues Native Americans face today?

GLOSSARY

activist: Someone who acts strongly in support of or against an issue.

ancestor: Someone who comes before others in their family tree.

demonstration: Politically, a public display of group feelings toward a person or cause.

discrimination: Treating some people unfairly because of things they can't control.

genocide: The deliberate destruction of a racial, political, or cultural group.

Indigenous: Describes the first people to live in an area.

massacre: The violent and cruel killing of people who are at an unfair disadvantage; also, to commit such a killing.

militant: Aggressive in support of a cause.

poverty: The state of being poor.

self-determination: The process by which a nation determines its own statehood and forms its own government.

treaty: A formal agreement between two groups of people.

FIND OUT MORE

Books

Braun, Eric. *The American Indian Rights Movement.* Minneapolis, MN: Lerner Publications, 2019.

Sorell, Traci. *We Are Still Here!: Native American Truths Everyone Should Know.* Watertown, MA: Charlesbridge, 2021.

Tudor, Aslan. *Young Native Activist: Growing Up in Native American Rights Movements.* Halifax, NS: EagleSpeaker Publishing, 2019.

Websites

CW Kids Ask: What Are American Indian People's Lives Like?
www.youtube.com/watch?v=305TQku5vKE
Three American Indians from different cultures answer questions from students.

Ducksters: Native American Rights
www.ducksters.com/history/civil_rights/native_american_rights.php
Learn more about the Indian Civil Rights Act of 1968.

Native Land
native-land.ca
This interactive map shows the traditional lands of Indigenous cultures around the world. Find out whose land you're living on today.

INDEX